The Pandavas

The Untold Story of Five Brothers Who Embarked on a Path of Destiny, Struggle, and Honor

Written By Tushar Paul

1

Introduction

In the grand land of Bharat, where rivers flowed like silver threads and mountains stood as ancient guardians, there lived a royal family whose legacy would shape the future of the world. This family, the Pandavas, consisted of five extraordinary brothers, each destined for greatness. Their childhood, filled with thrilling adventures, powerful lessons, and moments of joy and struggle, would lay the foundation for their legendary deeds that would echo through history.

In the magnificent kingdom of Hastinapura, the grand halls of the palace were alive with the sounds of learning and laughter. The *Pandavas*—Yudhishthira, Bhima, Arjuna, Nakula, and Sahadeva—were not just ordinary boys; they were the sons of kings and gods. Yudhishthira, the eldest, was blessed with the wisdom of Lord Yama, the god of justice. Bhima, the second-born, possessed the strength of the wind, a power that made him as mighty as a storm. Arjuna, the third prince, was granted the skill of archery from the god Indra, making him the greatest archer in the land. Nakula and Sahadeva, the twins, were renowned for their beauty, knowledge of horses, and wisdom.

Though they were born into royalty, their lives were not without challenges. As they grew in the palace, surrounded by luxury and care, they faced trials that would test their hearts, their strength, and their bond as brothers. Their cousins, the Kauravas, were always near, and the rivalry between them grew as the years passed. Yet, through every challenge, the Pandavas stood united, bound by an unbreakable bond of love, respect, and trust. They were not just brothers; they were best friends, companions on every adventure, and teammates through all of life's difficulties.

Their childhood was a time of discovery and growth, filled with moments of joy, laughter, and deep lessons. Whether it was Bhima's incredible strength that sometimes led to mischief, or Arjuna's unwavering focus during archery lessons, each day brought something new. Guided by wise mentors like the great Dronacharya and the fair King Bhishma, the Pandavas learned not only the ways of war but also the values of wisdom, leadership, and justice.

However, life at court was not always easy. The rivalry with their cousins brought its own set of challenges. Jealousy, anger, and misunderstandings often tested their unity. Yet, it was through these very trials that the Pandavas learned the most important lessons of all—about honor, family, and what it truly means to stand together in times of hardship.

As the brothers grew older, their courage and strength flourished. From their playful games to the serious moments of learning, they faced each challenge together. But they also began to see glimpses of their future roles as warriors and leaders, aware that the path ahead would not always be smooth. Despite this, they remained steadfast in their commitment to one another and to their people.

This is the story of the Pandavas childhood—filled with moments of laughter, challenges that tested their strength, and the timeless values of loyalty, courage, and friendship. Through these early adventures, they learned the lessons that would shape them into the heroes they were destined to become. It is a story of how unity, wisdom, and love can overcome even the greatest obstacles and how, as young princes, the Pandavas began to understand the true meaning of being leaders and warriors.

As you journey through the world of Hastinapura, you will witness the power of friendship, the strength of family, and the courage to face challenges head-on. The Pandavas childhood is just the beginning of a much larger tale, one that would change the course of history and inspire generations to come.

Chapter 1: The Princes of Hastinapura

The sun rose over the kingdom of Hastinapura, casting a warm, golden light over the magnificent city. It bathed the grand palace, towering above the courtyards, in its radiant glow. The air was filled with the songs of birds that fluttered from tree to tree, their melodious calls mixing with the distant sounds of the royal city waking up. It was a perfect day, one that promised something special for the children of the royal family—the *Pandavas*. Little did anyone know that this day would mark the beginning of a series of events that would change the future of Hastinapura and the very world itself.

Within the palace walls, the five Pandava brothers—Yudhishthira, Bhima, Arjuna, Nakula, and Sahadeva—woke up early, full of excitement. Today was no ordinary day. Today, they would take part in the grand archery competition hosted by their father, King Dhritarashtra, and the royal court. It was not only a contest of physical prowess, but a test of courage, skill, and character, and it was a day to prove themselves worthy of the royal legacy they were born into.

In the royal chamber, the eldest of the five brothers, Yudhishthira, was already awake, meditating in front of a small altar. His posture was calm, and his eyes were closed in deep concentration. Though only a child, Yudhishthira carried the wisdom of an elder. He had a quiet strength that came from his deep sense of responsibility, and a moral compass that guided his every decision. Yudhishthira was born to rule one day, and it was clear even then that he was the one who would carry the weight of the kingdom on his shoulders.

Beside him, his younger brother Bhima was already awake too, but unlike Yudhishthira, Bhima had no interest in meditation. Bhima was a powerhouse of energy and strength. Known for his boisterous nature, Bhima loved to wrestle, to compete, and to challenge anyone who came his way. His large frame and powerful muscles were a testament to his strength, a gift from the wind god, Vayu. Today, he could hardly contain his excitement. He had been looking forward to this day for weeks. The idea of competing in an archery contest, where strength could prove as important as skill, thrilled him.

Arjuna, the third-born, had his own quiet excitement. Unlike Bhima, Arjuna's strength lay not in his muscles, but in his unmatched skill with the bow and arrow. Arjuna had spent hours, days, and weeks practicing his archery with intense focus. His concentration was legendary, and his sharp eyes had already begun to see the world with the precision of an arrow's flight. He dreamed of becoming the greatest archer to ever live, a title that would be his one day, but he knew that to do so, he needed to face challenges like the one before him today.

Nakula and Sahadeva, the twins, were known for their wisdom, beauty, and grace. Though not as boisterous as Bhima or as focused as Arjuna, they were calm and collected, always ready to offer guidance to their brothers. Nakula's knowledge of horses was renowned, and Sahadeva's intelligence in other matters made them invaluable allies. They were known to complement each other, and their quiet wisdom made them highly respected by their family. Today, however, they were also excited to watch their brothers compete, and they shared a look of silent encouragement.

The royal palace was bustling with activity. The corridors echoed with the sounds of servants preparing the court for the competition, while nobles and warriors gathered to watch the contest. King Dhritarashtra, though blind, was seated on his royal throne, surrounded by attendants who described the events of the day in vivid detail. Beside him was Queen Gandhari, his wife, who had been blindfolded from birth and understood the world through her other senses. Together, they had raised the five princes with love and care, though the shadows of the royal family's politics always loomed over their hearts.

It was the first major public event where the princes would showcase their abilities, and both King Dhritarashtra and Queen Gandhari were eager to see how their sons would fare.

At the heart of the royal courtyard, a massive target was set up. It was no ordinary target—this was the famed wooden bird, known for its trickery and difficult movement. It was perched high above the ground on a rotating wheel, its wings spinning with incredible speed. The challenge was to shoot the bird's eye with a bow and arrow, and only the most skilled marksman would be able to succeed.

As the competition began, the royal announcer called the princes forward. The crowd of onlookers, nobles, warriors, and citizens, all eagerly awaited the moment when the Pandavas would display their prowess. The air was thick with excitement.

"Let the contest begin!" the announcer's voice rang out, and with a signal from the royal court, the princes took their positions.

First came Bhima. He stepped forward with confidence, his broad chest puffed out with pride. Bhima's strength was his greatest asset, but today, it was clear that strength alone would not be enough. Bhima aimed his bow at the rotating bird, his massive hands grasping the weapon with determination. He released the arrow with a grunt, but it flew off course, missing the bird entirely. The crowd fell silent, and even Bhima's face tightened in frustration.

"Don't worry, Bhima. You are strong, but you must learn patience and focus," Yudhishthira said, his voice calm and comforting.

Bhima looked at his older brother and grinned sheepishly. "I wanted to prove that strength matters," he said, "but I see now that it is not enough on its own."

Next came Arjuna. He was the one everyone had been waiting for. With a quiet and determined expression, Arjuna took his bow and arrow. His posture was perfect, his focus absolute. As the bird spun in the air, Arjuna's eyes followed it with unblinking precision. With a deep breath, he drew his bowstring back and released the arrow in one smooth motion. It flew through the air with unerring accuracy and struck the bird right in the eye. The target fell to the ground with a satisfying thud.

The crowd erupted into applause. King Dhritarashtra, though unable to see, could feel the energy in the air, and he smiled. "My son, Arjuna, has proven his skill," he said softly to Gandhari.

"I always knew he was destined for greatness," Gandhari replied, her voice full of pride.

Next came Yudhishthira's turn. The eldest Pandava was not a warrior like Bhima or Arjuna, but he had something far greater—wisdom. His ability to see beyond the surface, to read situations, and to use strategy was unmatched. Yudhishthira knew that this contest was not just about skill; it was about using one's mind. As the bird spun, Yudhishthira closed his eyes and focused deeply, trusting his instincts and his understanding of the world. He drew his bow and released his arrow with quiet confidence. The arrow flew, hitting the bird's eye perfectly.

The crowd was speechless. "A perfect shot," the announcer said in awe. "Such wisdom in action."

Yudhishthira stood, calm and composed, his eyes meeting those of his brothers. "We are all different, each with our own strengths," he said, his voice steady and full of quiet authority.

Bhima clapped him on the back. "That was impressive, Yudhishthira. You've shown us that wisdom is as powerful as strength."

Nakula and Sahadeva stood beside their brothers, their smiles warm. "You did well, Yudhishthira," Nakula said, his voice full of admiration.

As the competition ended and the day drew to a close, the Pandavas sat together, reflecting on the day's events. Despite their different strengths, each brother had proven their worth in their own way. The bond they shared was unbreakable, and it was clear that they would face many more challenges together.

Yudhishthira, always the wise one, looked at his brothers and said, "Today was not about winning or losing. It was about understanding who we are and what we can achieve together. We are not just princes; we are a family, and that is our greatest strength."

And so, as the sun set behind the palace, the five Pandava brothers walked together into the future, ready to face whatever challenges lay ahead. Their childhood had been one of learning and growing, but it was only the beginning of their incredible journey. Little did they know that the trials of life were just starting, and the lessons they would learn together would shape them into the heroes they were destined to become.

Chapter 2: The Secret Training Ground

The days following the archery competition were filled with excitement and discussion in the royal palace. While Arjuna's victory had brought him great praise and admiration, each of the Pandava brothers was more determined than ever to improve themselves. Bhima, who was known for his strength, wanted to become even stronger. Arjuna, having proven his skill with the bow, was already focused on perfecting his techniques. Yudhishthira, with his calm wisdom, knew the value of understanding one's self, while Nakula and Sahadeva, the twins, were eager to continue learning and growing in their respective fields of expertise.

Despite the cheers and celebrations, something else was brewing—a plan that would change the course of their lives. The young princes were eager to seek out their own paths and improve their skills beyond what the royal court could offer them. They had learned much under the guidance of their elders and teachers, but they felt a longing for something more—something secret, hidden away from the eyes of the court.

It was Yudhishthira, as always, who first brought up the idea. One evening, as the five brothers gathered in their private chamber to discuss their progress, he spoke with quiet determination.

"I have been thinking," Yudhishthira said, looking around at his brothers, "while the palace offers many lessons, we need to train in secret. We must challenge ourselves in ways the court cannot offer. Our destiny is not just to be princes; we must prepare ourselves for something greater. There is a hidden place, deep in the forest, where our true potential can be unlocked. I suggest we train there."

The idea caught everyone's attention, especially Bhima, whose enthusiasm was sparked by the notion of physical training far beyond what anyone in the palace could provide.

"Where is this secret place, Yudhishthira?" Bhima asked, his voice full of curiosity and excitement.

"It is a hidden grove, deep within the forest near the riverbanks. Only a few know of it, and its location is kept secret even from the royal court," Yudhishthira replied. "It is said to be a place where great warriors once trained—where both strength and skill were tested to the limits. If we are to grow into the warriors we are meant to be, this is the place."

Arjuna, whose quiet wisdom matched Yudhishthira's, nodded thoughtfully. "I agree. The forest is peaceful, and there, we will have no distractions, no prying eyes. Only our own training and the will to become greater than we are today."

Nakula, always a voice of reason, added, "But we must be cautious. If the court were to find out that we are training in secret, it could bring trouble. We must keep this between us, at least for now."

Sahadeva, the most introspective of the brothers, spoke next. "I've often wondered what lies beyond the palace walls. This might be our chance to truly test our limits, to grow into the men we are meant to be."

The five brothers made a pact that night, sealing their decision with the quiet promise of unity and shared purpose. They would train in secret, and no one in the court would know of their plans. It was a risky decision, but one that held the promise of great rewards.

The next morning, while the palace was still asleep and the kingdom was waking up to its usual rhythm, the Pandavas gathered in the stables, each wearing simple clothes to blend in. Yudhishthira, as the eldest, led the way, and each brother followed close behind. Their faces were determined, their steps firm, and their hearts were full of resolve.

They mounted their horses—each a gift from the royal stables—and rode out toward the forest. The path was long and winding, leading them through the outskirts of Hastinapura and into the thick woods that stretched for miles. The sounds of the palace slowly faded, replaced by the whispers of the wind and the rustling of the trees.

The forest was thick with dense foliage, and the air was heavy with the earthy scent of moss and wet leaves. As they rode deeper into the woods, the sunlight filtered through the branches above, creating a dappled pattern on the forest floor. The horses' hooves echoed through the stillness, and the brothers moved with purpose, eager to reach their destination.

After several hours of travel, they arrived at the hidden grove Yudhishthira had spoken of. It was a secluded spot, surrounded by ancient trees that stood like sentinels guarding the area. The ground was soft, covered with grass and moss, and a small, clear stream trickled nearby, its waters sparkling in the sunlight. The air was fresh, and there was a certain magic in the atmosphere, as if the land itself was alive with history.

"This is it," Yudhishthira said as he dismounted. "This is where we will train."

The brothers looked around in awe. The grove felt peaceful and sacred, a place untouched by time. It was clear that this was a special place—one where they would not only learn to sharpen their skills, but also to forge a deeper bond with one another.

They spent the rest of the day exploring the area and setting up camp. The grove had everything they needed: a clear space for practice, a stream for water, and shelter from the elements. The quiet of the forest made it the perfect place for reflection and growth.

The following morning, they began their training in earnest. Bhima, eager to test his strength, started by lifting massive stones from the riverbed and carrying them up and down the forest path. His muscles bulged as he lifted rock after rock, pushing himself harder and harder. His efforts were relentless, and he was determined to grow stronger than anyone could imagine.

Arjuna, on the other hand, set up a target near the clearing and began to practice his archery. His movements were swift and graceful, each shot hitting the mark with pinpoint precision. He focused on perfecting his technique, his bow and arrow becoming extensions of his will. With each arrow that flew, his confidence grew, and the brothers couldn't help but watch in awe.

Nakula and Sahadeva took to the more subtle arts. Nakula focused on training his horses, learning how to ride with unmatched agility and control. His bond with the horses grew stronger each day, and his skills became legendary. Sahadeva, with his natural intelligence, studied the land, learning how to track animals and navigate through the forest. His keen mind found patterns in nature that others might overlook.

Yudhishthira, ever the wise leader, focused on teaching his brothers the importance of balance. He knew that physical strength, skill, and wisdom had to coexist in harmony. Each day, he led them in meditation and reflection, teaching them how to listen to their hearts and minds, so that they could make decisions that would guide them through the challenges ahead.

Days turned into weeks, and the brothers grew stronger, wiser, and more skilled with every passing day. Their bond deepened as they trained together, supporting one another, pushing each other to be better. The forest, once quiet and still, now echoed with the sounds of their training—arrows flying through the air, Bhima's grunts as he lifted stones, and the rhythmic pounding of hooves on the forest floor.

But despite the peacefulness of the grove, the world outside continued to move forward. Back in Hastinapura, the royal court remained oblivious to the Pandavas' secret training. The kingdom's politics, intrigue, and rivalries continued to simmer, setting the stage for challenges that the brothers could never have imagined.

Though they were hidden away in the forest, the Pandavas' destiny was already unfolding. They were preparing not just for the contests and challenges of their childhood, but for the trials of their adulthood—the battles, the betrayals, and the decisions that would shape their future. In the heart of the forest, with each arrow that Arjuna loosed and each stone that Bhima lifted, they were unknowingly preparing for the greatest test of all: the battle of Kurukshetra, a war that would decide the fate of the entire world.

But for now, they were just five brothers, training together in secret, united in their quest for greatness.

Chapter 3: The Unseen Threat

The days in the secret grove passed quickly. Each day brought new challenges, both physical and mental. The Pandava brothers had become like a single, well-oiled machine—each supporting the other, pushing one another beyond their limits. They worked in perfect harmony, the unity between them growing stronger with each lesson learned.

Yet, despite the peacefulness of their hidden training ground, something dangerous was stirring in the world outside. The royal court of Hastinapura was far from the peaceful place it appeared to be. Whispered conversations, veiled plots, and the subtle undercurrents of political games filled the air, even if the Pandavas were unaware of them.

The eldest of the Kaurava brothers, Duryodhana, had grown more and more envious of the Pandavas. His resentment had always simmered beneath the surface, but now it was beginning to boil over. He had always coveted the throne of Hastinapura, and the rise of the Pandavas—especially their growing strength and the admiration they received from the people—had fueled his jealousy.

Duryodhana, along with his cousin and trusted ally Karna, had been watching the Pandavas' rise with suspicion. Although the Kauravas held the power in the kingdom, they knew that the Pandavas were destined for greatness, and that bothered Duryodhana immensely. The thought of five brothers, united in their purpose, growing stronger every day was a constant thorn in his side.

"Why does everyone adore them?" Duryodhana would grumble in the royal court. "It's as if they're destined to take everything that should rightfully be mine. The throne is mine by birthright! I am the true heir, not Yudhishthira!"

Karna, ever the loyal supporter of Duryodhana, often reminded him, "They may be strong, but remember, they are still under the shadow of your father's rule. They are just children, unaware of what lies ahead. You need not worry about them for now, my friend."

But Duryodhana's anger only grew. The more the Pandavas trained, the more his jealousy festered, and he decided that something had to be done to ensure that their growing influence would be stunted. He had already begun whispering lies about the Pandavas in the royal court, accusing them of acting against the family and the kingdom. He made sure his father, King Dhritarashtra, was aware of the supposed threats they posed.

Meanwhile, back in the hidden grove, the Pandava brothers were unaware of the brewing storm. They had become completely immersed in their training. Bhima's strength had surpassed even his expectations, and he had begun lifting boulders so large that even Arjuna was impressed.

Arjuna, in turn, had become a master of the bow. He could now shoot arrows that would split a falling leaf in mid-air. His determination had paid off, and he was starting to think that he could match the great archer, Parashurama, one day.

Nakula and Sahadeva had also honed their skills. Nakula's bond with horses had turned into something extraordinary—he could now control a herd with a mere look. Sahadeva's tracking skills had become legendary, and he was now able to find paths through the dense forest where others might have been lost.

Yudhishthira, ever the guide of his brothers, had perfected the art of mediation and focus. He had a calming influence on the group, always reminding them that they were not just training for power, but for wisdom and justice. They were learning not only the skills of warriors but the qualities of great leaders.

But despite their rapid progress, a shadow was creeping closer to them.

One day, as the brothers trained, a strange noise echoed through the forest—a distant sound that did not belong to the usual symphony of nature. Arjuna was the first to hear it. His sharp senses picked up the faint rustle of footsteps, too light to be the animals of the forest.

"Do you hear that?" he asked, looking around warily.

The other brothers immediately stopped their training and listened. The sound grew closer, the faint rustling turning into the sound of footsteps moving through the underbrush. Someone was out there.

Without hesitation, Yudhishthira raised his hand, signaling the group to remain silent. The brothers crouched low, blending into the shadows of the trees, their bodies tense, their senses alert. In the quiet stillness of the forest, they waited.

The noise drew closer and closer, and then, through the trees, a figure emerged—a tall man, dressed in simple but clean clothes, with a face that was hard to read. He looked as though he had been traveling for some time. His eyes scanned the area cautiously, and then he looked up, as though sensing that someone was watching him.

The Pandavas remained motionless. Arjuna had already drawn his bow silently, while Bhima's fists were clenched, ready to strike if needed.

The stranger, sensing something was wrong, began to walk more cautiously. As he moved closer to the clearing, he suddenly stopped. He had heard something—the faintest rustle of leaves as one of the brothers shifted slightly. His eyes narrowed, and he turned quickly in their direction.

The Pandavas didn't move. Yudhishthira, however, sensed the man wasn't an immediate threat. He stood up slowly, his presence calm and authoritative.

"Who are you?" Yudhishthira asked, his voice firm yet welcoming.

The man's eyes widened slightly, clearly startled by the sudden appearance of the young prince. For a moment, there was silence. The man hesitated, then stepped forward.

"I mean no harm," he said quickly. "I am a traveler, lost in these woods. I did not expect to find anyone here."

Yudhishthira studied the man carefully, reading his eyes. There was something strange about him, a familiarity that he couldn't quite place.

"Tell us your name," Bhima said, his voice booming.

The traveler paused before speaking. "I am called Rishabh," he replied. "I am a wanderer, traveling to distant lands in search of knowledge."

There was a long pause, and the brothers exchanged glances. A wanderer. That could mean anything. Still, there was no immediate danger, so Yudhishthira decided to let him speak.

"What knowledge do you seek?" Yudhishthira asked, his curiosity piqued.

Rishabh's eyes flickered with an unreadable expression, and then he spoke. "I seek to understand the great warriors of the past. Those who walked the path of greatness before us, and how they rose to power."

The Pandavas exchanged cautious looks. Was this man a messenger from the gods, or was he just another wanderer lost in the woods? Yudhishthira's instincts told him that this meeting was no coincidence. Their training, so carefully hidden, had now drawn the attention of someone—someone who might hold the key to understanding what awaited them on the horizon.

"I sense there is much more to your story, Rishabh," Yudhishthira said, studying him closely. "But for now, you will stay with us and break your fast. You have traveled far."

And so, the mysterious traveler stayed with them, though his presence lingered in the back of their minds like a faint echo of something yet to come. Unbeknownst to the Pandavas, Rishabh's arrival was not a mere coincidence. He was a harbinger of something much greater—a test, a challenge, or perhaps, a warning that the world beyond the forest was already watching them.

Chapter 4: The Secrets of the Sage

The morning after the mysterious traveler, Rishabh, had joined them, the air was still heavy with questions. The Pandavas were accustomed to challenges and surprises, but this man's arrival had unsettled them in ways they couldn't yet understand. They had agreed to allow him to stay, but the brothers' keen instincts told them that Rishabh was no ordinary wanderer.

As they gathered around the small campfire that morning, Yudhishthira was the first to speak, breaking the silence that hung over the group.

"Rishabh, tell us more about your travels," he said gently, his voice calm but curious. "What brings you to these forests, and what knowledge do you seek from us?"

Rishabh looked up, his deep-set eyes scanning the horizon as though he were looking for something. He did not immediately answer, but his face bore an expression of contemplation. The winds rustled the trees around them, filling the silence with a calming sound that made the moment feel more profound.

Finally, the sage spoke, his voice steady and full of wisdom. "I have wandered many lands," he began, "seeking the ancient wisdom of the world, and I have met many kings, sages, and warriors. But what I seek now is something greater—something that can only be found by those who have the courage to shape the future, not just follow the past."

Arjuna, who had been quietly listening, felt a stir of excitement. He was always eager to learn more about what lay beyond his own skills with the bow and the art of war.

"Greatness?" Arjuna asked, leaning forward. "What does it mean to shape the future? Is it only through strength and skill that one becomes great, or is there something more?"

Rishabh turned his gaze to Arjuna, a slight smile on his lips. "It is not strength alone, young prince, that defines greatness. It is the heart and mind of a warrior, the wisdom of a king, and the compassion of a true leader. Only when all these elements come together can one truly shape the future."

The brothers exchanged looks, absorbing the sage's words. Bhima, the ever-impulsive and fiercely strong one, was the first to speak up.

"But how can wisdom and compassion defeat an enemy?" Bhima asked, his tone skeptical. "Our strength is what has always brought us victory. We have trained ourselves to be the greatest warriors, and our power is unmatched!"

Rishabh's smile remained, as if he had expected this response. He shook his head slowly, the calmness in his demeanor never faltering.

"Strength is indeed a part of the equation," he said softly, "but it is not the whole. Your strength is a reflection of your inner resolve, but it is your mind that will guide it, and your heart that will determine how it is used. Think of the great warriors and kings of the past. Some were strong, but many of them were not as strong as you. Yet they were able to rule, to protect, and to win battles. Why?"

The question hung in the air like a riddle, and for the first time in days, the brothers fell into deep thought. Yudhishthira, always the contemplative one, was the first to speak.

"Is it wisdom, then? The ability to make the right decisions?" he asked, his voice soft yet filled with curiosity.

Rishabh nodded. "Exactly. The greatest strength comes not from the body, but from the mind. A true warrior knows when to fight and when to show mercy. A true leader knows how to unite people for a greater cause. And a true king knows how to balance justice and compassion."

For the first time, the brothers realized that Rishabh was not here just to train them physically, but to offer them a deeper understanding of what it meant to wield their strength wisely.

As the morning wore on, the brothers sat in silence, digesting the sage's words. Each of them knew, deep down, that this was only the beginning of something far greater than just their training in the forest.

That afternoon, Rishabh took them to a hidden clearing deeper in the forest, a place they had never ventured before. The trees here were ancient, their trunks thick with age, and the air was thick with a sense of reverence. In the center of the clearing was a large, flat stone, carved with intricate symbols that none of the brothers recognized.

"This," Rishabh said, gesturing to the stone, "is an ancient altar. It has been here long before you were born, and it will remain long after you leave. This is a place of wisdom, a place where the past and future meet. Only those who are truly ready to understand the mysteries of the world will be able to decipher the meaning of the symbols that lie upon this stone."

The brothers stepped forward, their eyes wide with awe. Arjuna was the first to reach the stone, his hands brushing over the carved symbols. He could feel an energy emanating from the surface, as though the very stone was alive with the history of ages past.

"What do they mean?" Arjuna asked, his voice full of wonder.

Rishabh stepped forward, his fingers brushing against the symbols as well. "These symbols are the language of the gods. They hold the key to many of the secrets of the world—secrets of power, knowledge, and destiny. But only those who are truly ready to understand will be able to see the truth."

Yudhishthira stepped forward, his brow furrowed in concentration. "How can we know if we are ready?" he asked, his voice filled with uncertainty.

Rishabh turned to face him, his eyes deep and wise. "You are already ready," he said. "The very fact that you are here, seeking knowledge and training, means that you are ready to understand what others cannot. But remember, the knowledge you seek is not for the sake of power alone. It is for the sake of those you will one day rule, those who will look to you for guidance. It is for them that you must seek wisdom, not for yourself."

The brothers stood in silence for a moment, each one reflecting on the words of the sage. They understood, at last, that their journey was not only one of physical training but also one of spiritual and mental growth. They had been chosen for something greater, and the path ahead would be difficult, but they knew they must walk it together.

As the sun began to set, casting long shadows across the clearing, Rishabh turned to leave, signaling that their time at the altar was drawing to a close.

"Remember," he said, his voice carrying the weight of ages. "The knowledge of the gods is not easily understood, but it will guide you when the time comes. Be patient, for the world is not yet ready for the greatness you will one day possess."

The brothers stood in silence as the sage disappeared into the trees, his figure vanishing as if he had never been there at all. The air around them felt charged, as if the very forest was alive with ancient power.

They knew, without a doubt, that their journey had only just begun.

Chapter 5: Trials of Strength and Wisdom

The days that followed were filled with a steady rhythm—early mornings spent in the forest with Rishabh, practicing their skills and learning lessons of wisdom, and late afternoons immersed in quiet reflection by the campfire. The Pandavas had grown accustomed to Rishabh's presence, and though the sage's teachings were often cryptic and deep, they had begun to see a pattern in his words and actions. There was a method to his madness, an underlying truth to everything he said. And slowly, the brothers began to understand that their journey would not only be one of physical prowess, but also one of mental and spiritual growth.

One day, as the morning sun peeked through the canopy of trees, casting golden beams of light upon the forest floor, Rishabh called them together at the edge of a clearing. The air was crisp and cool, and the leaves rustled with the promise of something new.

"Today," Rishabh announced, his voice calm yet commanding, "you will face your first true trial."

The brothers exchanged curious looks. They had been training for weeks now, growing stronger, faster, and more disciplined, but they had not yet encountered a challenge that truly tested their mettle. They had been preparing for something, but none of them knew exactly what it would be.

"What kind of trial, Rishabh?" asked Arjuna, his brow furrowing with both excitement and anticipation.

"You will face an enemy," Rishabh replied, a slight smile playing on his lips. "But this enemy will not be a mere mortal. It will be a reflection of yourselves—your fears, your doubts, your weaknesses. You will each face this trial alone, and only when you conquer it will you be ready to advance."

Bhima, ever the eager one, clenched his fists, ready for whatever challenge awaited them. "An enemy of our own?" he asked, his voice a mixture of confusion and determination. "What do you mean, Rishabh?"

Rishabh nodded. "You will soon understand. You each have something inside you that holds you back, something that limits your true potential. This trial will reveal it, and only by overcoming it will you learn the true nature of your strength."

With a wave of his hand, Rishabh gestured to the center of the clearing. The air seemed to shift as the ground beneath them hummed with energy. Slowly, out of the earth, dark shadows began to take shape, swirling like smoke in the wind. The brothers stood frozen in place as the shadows coalesced into solid forms, and before them stood a figure, an enemy unlike any they had ever seen.

It was a mirror image of each of them.

Yudhishthira's doppelganger stood tall and regal, his eyes cold and calculating. His posture was perfect, a reflection of the wisdom and discipline that Yudhishthira himself embodied, but there was something unsettling about the figure. It was as if the reflection of his righteous path had taken on a darker, more controlling form.

Arjuna's reflection was as precise and focused as his own skills with the bow, but there was a flicker of arrogance in his eyes—an unsettling reminder of the pride that sometimes clouded his judgment.

Bhima's doppelganger was larger and more imposing, his muscles rippling with raw strength. But his expression was filled with rage, as though he could not control the ferocity within him, a reflection of Bhima's sometimes reckless anger.

Nakula and Sahadeva, the twins, faced reflections that mirrored their beauty and grace, but there was something deceptive in their expressions. The shadows in their eyes hinted at jealousy and self-doubt, emotions that the brothers had not fully acknowledged in themselves.

The brothers stood in silence, taken aback by the sight before them. These were not enemies to be fought with swords or spears. These were the dark sides of themselves—their inner struggles, fears, and imperfections.

"You must face your reflection," Rishabh's voice echoed, cutting through the stillness. "Only by conquering the part of yourself that holds you back can you move forward. This is not a battle of strength, but a battle of the heart and mind."

Without another word, the shadowy figures advanced.

Yudhishthira's Trial: The Struggle for Control

Yudhishthira stepped forward, his eyes locked on his reflection. He felt a surge of unease, the coldness of the figure mirroring his every movement. His reflection's gaze was piercing, almost accusatory, as if it was judging him for every decision he had made.

"Do you truly believe you are the rightful king?" the reflection asked in a voice that was eerily similar to his own. "Are you not just a puppet, following the rules and pretending to be righteous?"

Yudhishthira stood tall, his heart racing. The reflection's words struck a nerve, as they were his own doubts manifested. Was he too rigid in his sense of justice? Had he become a ruler who placed too much emphasis on the rules and not enough on the heart of the people?

"You will never lead with true wisdom, Yudhishthira," the reflection continued. "You are afraid to act when it matters, too focused on what is right rather than what is necessary."

Yudhishthira clenched his fists. He knew that his sense of righteousness was his greatest strength, but he also understood that sometimes, being a good king meant making difficult decisions, even when they were not entirely just. He had to accept that not every choice would be easy, and that sometimes, the path of wisdom required him to balance justice with compassion.

"I am not afraid to lead," Yudhishthira said firmly. "I will lead with both wisdom and compassion, and I will make the hard choices when they are needed."

With that, his reflection dissipated into the air, vanishing as quickly as it had appeared.

Arjuna's Trial: Overcoming Arrogance

Next, Arjuna faced his reflection, which stood poised with a bow, its arrow aimed at an unseen target. The figure's eyes burned with a sense of superiority, a trait that Arjuna had battled within himself for years.

"You think you are the greatest warrior in the world, don't you?" the reflection taunted. "You think your skills with the bow make you invincible."

Arjuna felt his heart tighten, as the reflection's words echoed his own pride. He had always been known for his unrivaled skill with the bow, and for a long time, he had believed that this alone made him the greatest of all warriors. But was this arrogance? Did he truly see himself as superior to others?

"You are nothing without humility," the reflection sneered. "Your pride will be your downfall."

Arjuna took a deep breath, the weight of the words pressing down on him. He had often struggled with pride, especially in the face of his victories. But now, he understood that true strength lay not only in his ability to fight, but in his ability to remain humble in the face of greatness.

"I am more than my skill with the bow," Arjuna said, his voice calm but resolute. "I will fight with humility and honor, and I will remember that there is always more to learn, even for the greatest of warriors."

His reflection flickered and then dissolved, leaving only a stillness in its wake.

The Trials of Bhima, Nakula, and Sahadeva

Bhima's reflection roared with anger, an embodiment of the fierce, untamed power that often consumed him. It charged at him with all the strength and fury he could muster, but Bhima held his ground. He knew that his strength was his greatest asset, but also his greatest weakness. He could no longer let his anger control him.

Nakula and Sahadeva, standing side by side, faced reflections that whispered doubts into their hearts—feelings of jealousy and insecurity that they had never fully acknowledged. They struggled with their place in the world, always in the shadow of their elder brothers. But as they fought their reflections, they realized that their bond, their shared strengths, were enough to overcome their self-doubt.

The trials were not easy, but one by one, the Pandavas faced their inner demons, conquering the weaknesses that had held them back. And with each victory, they grew stronger, not just in body, but in spirit.

When the trials were over, Rishabh appeared once again, his expression proud.

"You have faced the greatest enemy of all," he said. "Yourself. And you have won. But remember, this is just the beginning. There will be many more trials ahead, but now you are ready."

The brothers stood together, their hearts and minds clearer than they had ever been. They had learned something invaluable that day—not just about their own strength, but about the strength of wisdom, humility, and self-awareness. And with this newfound knowledge, they knew that they could face whatever challenges the future held.

Chapter 6: The Divine Gift

The days after their trials were filled with reflection and quiet moments of growth. The Pandavas had learned lessons that would shape their futures, and Rishabh's teachings had planted seeds of wisdom in their hearts. They had grown stronger, not just physically, but in their understanding of themselves and their place in the world. Yet, deep down, the brothers knew that their journey was far from over. There was still so much to learn, so many paths to explore.

One morning, as the sun cast its first rays over the horizon, the air in the forest felt different. There was a quiet stillness, as though nature itself was holding its breath. The Pandavas, now accustomed to the rhythm of the forest, were sitting by the riverbank, their thoughts drifting like the current of the water before them.

Rishabh approached them, his steps soft and measured. He had a different air about him today, one that carried a sense of purpose and urgency.

"Brothers," Rishabh began, his voice gentle but firm, "today, you will receive a gift, one that will aid you in the trials to come. It is a gift that will set you apart and help you on your path. But remember, this gift is not for you alone. It is a tool—a means to fulfill your destiny."

The brothers turned to look at him, curiosity and excitement in their eyes. They had faced many challenges, and now it seemed as though Rishabh was preparing to grant them something even more powerful.

"What kind of gift, Rishabh?" Yudhishthira asked, his voice filled with anticipation.

Rishabh did not answer immediately. Instead, he gestured for them to follow him. They rose from the riverbank and walked deeper into the forest, following their sage guide as he led them to a secluded grove.

In the center of the grove stood an ancient tree, its trunk gnarled and twisted with age. Its roots stretched deep into the earth, and its branches reached high toward the sky, as though trying to touch the heavens. The tree exuded a quiet, powerful energy, and the brothers could feel the weight of its presence.

"This tree," Rishabh said, "is sacred. It has stood here for centuries, and it holds within it the power of the divine. It is from this tree that you will receive the gifts that will guide you."

The Pandavas stood in awe as Rishabh raised his arms toward the sky, his voice carrying the weight of ancient words. The wind began to stir, and the leaves of the tree rustled as if answering his call. There was a moment of stillness, and then, as if the tree itself had heard Rishabh's invocation, a golden light began to emanate from its trunk.

Slowly, from the heart of the tree, five distinct objects began to emerge— each glowing with divine energy. One by one, the objects floated toward the brothers, who watched in silent wonder.

Rishabh spoke again, his voice low and reverent. "These are your gifts, each one tailored to your strengths and your path. Take them, and understand their significance."

The Gift for Yudhishthira

The first object to float toward Yudhishthira was a golden crown, adorned with intricate designs and set with precious stones that glinted in the light. It was a crown that gleamed with wisdom, a symbol of leadership, and a reminder of the weight of responsibility that Yudhishthira would one day bear.

"This crown," Rishabh explained, "is a symbol of your destiny to lead. It is not merely an ornament, but a reminder of the responsibility that comes with leadership. It will grant you wisdom in times of doubt and clarity in moments of decision. But remember, it is your heart and your integrity that will make you a true king, not the crown itself."

Yudhishthira took the crown in his hands, feeling its weight. It was light, yet the responsibility it carried seemed immense. He bowed his head in reverence, understanding the path that lay ahead of him.

The Gift for Arjuna

Next, a bow appeared before Arjuna, radiant and strong. The bow was unlike any other he had seen, with a curved, polished surface that seemed to shimmer with divine energy. The string, made of golden thread, hummed with power. It was a weapon that embodied his skill, but also his focus and determination.

"This bow," Rishabh said, "is a gift of precision and mastery. It will enhance your abilities and allow you to strike with unparalleled accuracy. But remember, true power lies not in the weapon, but in the mind that wields it. This bow will guide your hand, but it is your heart that will guide your aim."

Arjuna reached out and took the bow in his hands, feeling its power course through him. He knew that his path as a warrior was far from over, and that this gift would be a vital part of the challenges that lay ahead.

The Gift for Bhima

For Bhima, the gift was a mace, crafted from an unearthly metal that glowed with an inner fire. It was heavy, yet perfectly balanced, designed for the brute strength that Bhima possessed. The mace hummed with energy, as if it had a life of its own, waiting for its master to wield it.

"This mace," Rishabh explained, "represents the power and strength that you possess. It will amplify your might, but remember—strength is not just about physical power. True strength comes from control, from the ability to temper your anger and use your strength wisely."

Bhima took the mace in his hands, his heart swelling with pride. He knew that his physical power was unmatched, but Rishabh's words reminded him that strength was not just about force; it was about how he chose to use it.

The Gift for Nakula

For Nakula, the gift was a pair of golden horseshoes, shining brightly in the sunlight. They were designed to fit perfectly around his feet, enhancing his speed and agility. The horseshoes were as light as a feather, yet they carried an aura of unparalleled grace.

"These horseshoes," Rishabh said, "will grant you unmatched speed and agility. But they are also a reminder that beauty and grace are as powerful as strength. The path you walk will not always be easy, but your grace will allow you to navigate it with ease."

Nakula took the horseshoes and slipped them onto his feet, feeling a surge of energy flow through him. He knew that his speed and agility would be tested in ways he could not yet imagine, but this gift would guide him as he moved forward.

The Gift for Sahadeva

The final gift, for Sahadeva, was a sword of gleaming silver, its blade sharp and flawless. The sword was not just a weapon, but an instrument of clarity and precision. The hilt was carved with intricate designs, symbolizing wisdom and insight.

"This sword," Rishabh explained, "represents your intelligence and your ability to discern truth from falsehood. It will sharpen your mind and allow you to cut through confusion. But remember, wisdom is not just about knowledge; it is about the wisdom to know when to act and when to wait."

Sahadeva took the sword in his hands, feeling its power and clarity. He understood that while the sword could help him in battle, it was his mind that would be his true weapon.

The Brothers Unite

With their gifts in hand, the Pandavas stood together, united not just by blood, but by the divine tools that would help them fulfill their destinies. Rishabh smiled at them, his eyes filled with pride.

"These gifts are not just objects," he said. "They are symbols of your strengths, your paths, and your responsibilities. Use them wisely, for they will guide you through the challenges to come. But remember, the greatest gift you possess is not the crown, the bow, the mace, the horseshoes, or the sword. It is your unity as brothers. Together, you are stronger than any weapon, and together, you will overcome all obstacles."

The Pandavas looked at one another, their hearts filled with gratitude and determination. They knew that the journey ahead would be filled with trials, but with the gifts they had received and the bond they shared, they were ready to face whatever challenges came their way.

As the golden light from the tree faded, the brothers turned to Rishabh, their hearts full of resolve. They had been given the tools, but now it was up to them to shape their destinies.

And with that, they stepped forward, together, ready to embark on the next chapter of their journey.

Chapter 7: The Test of Courage

The days following their divine gifts were marked with a renewed sense of purpose and preparation. The Pandavas knew that their path was fraught with challenges, and that each gift they had received came with its own responsibility. The forest, once a place of peace and refuge, now seemed to stir with the whisper of distant trials, as if nature itself was preparing to test their resolve.

Rishabh, ever watchful and wise, gathered the brothers one evening as the stars began to twinkle in the darkening sky. They sat around a small fire, its warm light flickering against the cool night air. The flames danced as though eager to share a secret, and the night seemed to hold its breath, waiting for the sage to speak.

"Brothers," Rishabh began, his voice calm yet filled with the weight of his knowledge, "you have received the gifts of strength, wisdom, grace, and courage, each one forged to assist you in your journey. But these gifts will not be enough if you do not also learn the most important lesson of all—the test of courage."

The brothers looked at one another, sensing that this lesson would be different from any they had faced before. The Pandavas, though young, had already experienced their share of trials, but courage was something more intangible, more elusive. It was not just about the ability to fight or to endure hardship; it was about standing firm in the face of fear, about rising up when everything around you seems impossible.

Rishabh continued, his eyes fixed on each of them in turn. "Courage is not the absence of fear. It is the strength to stand tall despite it. To face the unknown and press forward, knowing that the road ahead is dark and uncertain. Only when you can summon courage in the face of your deepest fears will you truly be ready to face your destiny."

The brothers sat silently, their minds turning over Rishabh's words. They knew that they would have to confront challenges that would test their mettle, both as individuals and as a united force.

Rishabh smiled softly as he watched their thoughtful expressions. "There is a place deep within this forest, a place of shadows and uncertainty. It is known as the Shadow Grove. There, you will be tested. It is not an easy journey, and many who have entered have returned with their spirits shaken. But you will go as a family, for together, you will find the strength to face the darkness that lies ahead."

The brothers exchanged looks, a silent understanding passing between them. This was not just a test of physical strength; it was a test of their hearts, their unity, and their resolve.

The next morning, they set out for the Shadow Grove, their hearts heavy with both anticipation and trepidation. The forest around them seemed to close in, the trees towering overhead as if watching their every step. The air grew cooler as they ventured deeper, and the once vibrant sounds of the forest quieted. It was as if the very life of the forest had retreated, leaving behind an eerie silence.

As they neared the grove, the atmosphere grew thick with an unsettling stillness. The path became narrow, winding, and shadowed, and the brothers felt a chill creep over them. Their steps slowed as they moved deeper into the darkness. Each sound—each snap of a twig beneath their feet—seemed amplified in the quiet.

Finally, they reached the entrance of the grove, a place where the light barely penetrated, and the shadows seemed to twist and coil like living things. The trees here were ancient, their bark twisted and gnarled, their branches heavy with the weight of forgotten memories.

Rishabh stood at the edge of the grove, his eyes scanning the dark path ahead. "This is the place," he said. "Here, your courage will be tested. You will face fears you cannot see, and challenges you cannot predict. But remember this: in the shadows, you will find your true strength. The darkness is not your enemy—it is your mirror. What you fear most will reveal the truth about who you are."

The brothers exchanged uncertain glances, but Rishabh's steady presence gave them the courage they needed. One by one, they stepped into the grove, the darkness closing around them like a heavy blanket.

At first, the grove seemed empty, as though they had entered a world devoid of life. But as they walked deeper, the shadows began to shift, and strange shapes began to emerge from the corners of their vision. At first, they were only fleeting glimpses—figures moving in the darkness, faces that vanished when they tried to focus on them. But the deeper they ventured, the more tangible the fears became.

Yudhishthira was the first to feel the weight of his fear. As they walked through the grove, he suddenly felt a sense of isolation, as if he were alone in the world. The faces of his family seemed to blur, and the path ahead became uncertain. His heart raced as he struggled to find his bearings, but the fear of failure, of leading his brothers into danger, consumed him. For a moment, he felt the overwhelming pressure of his future responsibility.

But then, he remembered Rishabh's words. "Courage is not the absence of fear, but the strength to move forward despite it." He took a deep breath, grounded himself, and reached out for his brothers. Together, they pressed on, Yudhishthira finding the strength to guide them through the uncertainty.

Arjuna, too, faced his own fear in the grove. As he moved through the shadows, he was confronted by illusions of his past battles—his failures, his doubts, the moments when he had questioned his ability as a warrior. The fear of not living up to his potential, of failing those who relied on him, threatened to consume him.

But then, the weight of the bow he carried reminded him of his true purpose. He had been born to fight, to protect, and to serve. He gripped the bow tightly, letting its strength remind him of his own. He was not alone in this journey, and he would not falter. With a steady hand and a focused mind, Arjuna pushed forward, his courage shining through the shadows.

For Bhima, the grove manifested his fear of losing control. The shadows seemed to mock his strength, showing him a world where his power was not enough to protect those he loved. He was surrounded by illusions of his enemies, creatures far stronger than any he had faced. The anger that rose within him threatened to overtake his mind, but he remembered Rishabh's lesson—that true strength came from control, not from blind fury.

Bhima closed his eyes, centered himself, and focused on his breath. The anger subsided, and he was able to move forward, his heart calm and resolute. He realized that his strength was not just in his muscles, but in his ability to maintain control when faced with the chaos of the world.

Nakula and Sahadeva, too, faced their own fears in the grove. For Nakula, it was the fear of being overlooked, of being seen as less important than his brothers. For Sahadeva, it was the fear of not being able to live up to the wisdom that had been bestowed upon him. But in the shadows, they found clarity. Nakula realized that his speed and grace were not just tools of battle; they were his unique gifts, and they made him special. Sahadeva understood that his wisdom would only grow with time, and that his path was his own to forge.

Together, the Pandavas walked through the shadows, their courage growing with each step. They emerged from the grove not as individuals, but as a unified force, their hearts stronger, their minds clearer, and their spirits unshaken.

As they stepped back into the light, Rishabh was waiting for them. His smile was one of pride, but there was something else in his eyes—a deep respect for the journey they had just completed.

"You have faced the darkness and emerged stronger," he said. "This test was not just to challenge your courage, but to show you that the light is not found by avoiding the shadows. It is found by embracing them and moving forward, no matter how uncertain the path may seem."

The Pandavas stood together, their bond unbreakable, their hearts filled with a newfound strength. They had passed the test of courage, and though the road ahead was still fraught with trials, they knew that they were ready for whatever came next.

Chapter 8: The Power of Unity

The days following the test in the Shadow Grove were filled with a quiet strength. The Pandavas felt a sense of accomplishment in their hearts, knowing they had faced their fears and emerged stronger. But even in their triumph, there was an unspoken awareness that their journey was only beginning. Though their courage had been tested, they were now preparing for a different kind of challenge—one that would test their unity.

Rishabh, always the guiding force in their lives, noticed the subtle changes in the brothers. There was a quiet understanding between them now, a new strength in their bond, but Rishabh also sensed that there were still unresolved tensions between them. The bonds of brotherhood were strong, but each of them had their own strengths and weaknesses, and at times, these differences threatened to pull them apart.

One morning, as the first light of dawn filtered through the trees, Rishabh gathered the Pandavas by the riverbank. The air was fresh, the water sparkling under the sun's early rays, and the sounds of the forest seemed to hum in anticipation.

"Brothers," Rishabh began, his voice calm but firm, "you have proven your individual courage. But there is another lesson yet to learn. A lesson that will prove far more difficult than facing the darkness of the Shadow Grove. It is the lesson of unity. A house divided will never stand. A force divided can never prevail. You must learn to work together—not just as brothers, but as a single, united force."

The words hung in the air, the weight of them sinking into the hearts of the Pandavas. They had been tested individually, but now, for the first time, they would face a trial that would test their ability to function as one.

"To truly understand the power of unity," Rishabh continued, "you must first learn the art of balance. Each of you has a unique strength, but no single strength is enough to face the trials ahead. It is only when you combine your gifts, when you learn to support one another, that you will truly become unstoppable."

The brothers looked at each other, a mixture of uncertainty and resolve in their eyes. They were each so different—Yudhishthira, the wise and just leader; Bhima, the strong and fearless warrior; Arjuna, the skilled archer and strategist; Nakula and Sahadeva, the twins whose grace and wisdom completed the circle. It seemed as though each brother was a pillar on his own, but the true test would be whether they could stand together as one.

Rishabh's gaze softened as he surveyed the brothers. "Your task is simple," he said, "but not easy. You will journey through the forest, to the other side of the river. Along the way, you will encounter challenges that you can only overcome by working together. If even one of you falters, the whole group will fail. Remember, each strength has its place, but it is only when all of your strengths combine that you will succeed."

Without another word, Rishabh turned and began walking toward the dense forest, signaling for the Pandavas to follow. The brothers hesitated for a moment, but then, with a shared glance, they fell into step behind their mentor.

The journey through the forest was more challenging than any of them could have imagined. As they ventured deeper, the terrain grew rougher, and the path became more treacherous. Dense underbrush scratched at their skin, and the air grew thick with humidity. But the physical challenge was only the beginning.

Soon, the brothers found themselves standing at the edge of a deep ravine, its chasm too wide to cross by jumping, too deep to climb. Across the ravine was a narrow stone bridge, but it was unstable, swaying with each gust of wind. The task was clear—cross the ravine, but how?

Yudhishthira stepped forward, his mind already assessing the situation. "We will need to support each other. Bhima and Arjuna can go first, securing the path, while Nakula and Sahadeva will help me carry the weaker ones across."

At first, the plan seemed simple enough. Bhima, with his great strength, was the first to step onto the bridge. The others watched with bated breath as the bridge swayed beneath his feet, creaking ominously. His muscles strained with each step, but he kept moving forward, his eyes fixed on the other side.

Once Bhima crossed, Arjuna followed, his steady movements a testament to his control and skill. As the last two brothers prepared to cross, Nakula and Sahadeva, it became clear that the bridge was barely strong enough to hold them. The next steps would be critical.

It was at this moment that the brothers realized the true meaning of Rishabh's lesson. If any one of them hesitated, the bridge would collapse under the strain. Their combined weight, their combined efforts, were needed to keep the bridge from giving way.

Nakula, who was quick and agile, took the lead next, his footfalls light yet sure. Sahadeva followed close behind, their movements in perfect sync. When the last of them reached the other side, they could all breathe a sigh of relief. The bridge had held, not because of their individual strength, but because of their unity and trust in one another.

"Well done," Rishabh's voice rang out from the other side of the ravine, his tone warm with approval. "This is the strength of unity—each brother bringing his unique gift to the task, supporting one another when the challenge seems insurmountable."

The brothers paused, taking in the significance of the moment. They had crossed the ravine not through brute force, but through cooperation and trust. They realized that their strength lay not in competing with each other, but in complementing one another.

Their journey continued, and the lessons of unity kept unfolding before them. There were times when one brother's skill was needed to overcome an obstacle—Yudhishthira's wisdom guiding them when they encountered tricky situations, Arjuna's precision and strategy solving problems from afar, Bhima's strength moving boulders or breaking barriers, and Nakula and Sahadeva's agility and resourcefulness finding paths where others saw none.

Each trial was more difficult than the last, but each time they succeeded, their bond grew stronger. They learned that every challenge could be faced as long as they were united, and that the power of their unity was greater than any individual strength they possessed.

By the time they returned to their starting point, the brothers were not just a family—they were a team, a force to be reckoned with. They had learned that no obstacle could stand in their way when they worked together, and their confidence in each other was unshakeable.

As the sun began to set, painting the sky with hues of pink and gold, Rishabh spoke once more. "Remember this lesson, my sons. The world will test you in many ways, but it is your unity that will see you through. When you stand together, no challenge is too great. And with this strength, you will fulfill your destiny."

The Pandavas stood in silence, their hearts full of newfound understanding. They had learned that their true strength did not lie in their individual abilities, but in their ability to come together as one. The road ahead was still long, and the trials would continue, but they knew now that as long as they stood together, nothing could defeat them.

And so, with renewed purpose, they continued their journey, united as
brothers and stronger than ever.

Chapter 9: The Trial of the Elements

The Pandavas' journey through the forest had been full of lessons, each one more challenging than the last. After the trial of unity, where they had learned to rely on each other's strengths, Rishabh now had another lesson in store. It was a test that would stretch their minds and bodies to the limits. It was the Trial of the Elements.

One morning, as the sun barely kissed the horizon, Rishabh gathered the brothers once again. They were standing near a large, ancient tree whose roots sprawled across the ground like veins in the earth. The air was thick with a sense of anticipation.

"Today," Rishabh began, his voice steady, "you will face the Trial of the Elements. This is a trial that will test your ability to adapt, to endure, and to master the four fundamental forces of nature—earth, water, fire, and air."

The brothers exchanged uncertain glances. Each of them had their own strengths, but none of them had faced a challenge that involved such a broad range of elements. What did it mean to master the forces of nature?

Rishabh continued, "Each element holds a lesson. Earth teaches resilience and stability, water teaches adaptability and flow, fire teaches transformation and courage, and air teaches freedom and clarity. You must prove your worth in each trial, and only then will you be ready to face the true challenges of your destiny."

With no more explanation, Rishabh pointed to the forest in front of them. "The trial begins now. Follow me."

The Pandavas followed Rishabh as he led them to a clearing. The ground beneath their feet was solid and dry, the trees surrounding them dense and towering. The air seemed charged, almost alive, and the brothers could feel the weight of the moment. Rishabh stepped into the center of the clearing, motioning for them to follow.

"The first trial is Earth," he said. "You will need to move this boulder." He pointed to a massive rock that lay in the center of the clearing, large enough to fill the space between the brothers. "But you must do so without brute strength. Instead, you must focus on stability and resilience. Work with the earth, not against it."

The Pandavas gathered around the boulder. At first, Bhima, being the strongest of the brothers, stepped forward. He tried to lift the rock, using all his might. He gritted his teeth, his muscles straining, but the rock barely budged.

"Stop," Rishabh called gently. "This is not about strength. This is about understanding the earth's power."

The brothers stepped back and looked at the rock with new eyes. It was not something to force, but something to respect. Yudhishthira, always the wise one, knelt down and placed his hands on the earth. He felt the solid ground beneath him, the vibrations of the earth, its stability. Slowly, he began to focus on the energy of the rock, visualizing its connection to the earth. The others joined him, placing their hands on the ground and focusing on the stillness.

After several moments of quiet concentration, Yudhishthira stood up. "Try again," he said to Bhima.

Bhima placed his hands on the rock, not with force, but with a calm and steady touch. He imagined the earth's strength flowing through him, grounding him. Together, with Nakula and Sahadeva guiding him, they worked in unison, and finally, with a slow, deliberate push, the rock shifted.

"Well done," Rishabh said with a proud smile. "You have learned the power of earth: resilience, patience, and the ability to find stability even in the most challenging situations."

The brothers were filled with a sense of accomplishment. They had overcome their first trial, but the trials of water, fire, and air still lay ahead.

They followed Rishabh to the next part of the forest, where a swift, sparkling river cut through the landscape. The sound of rushing water filled the air, creating a peaceful yet powerful atmosphere.

"Next, you must face the Trial of Water," Rishabh said. "Water is not about resistance, but adaptability. It flows, it bends, it finds a way forward no matter the obstacle. You must cross this river, but you may not use force. Instead, you must use your minds and your understanding of the flow."

The river was wide, and its currents were strong. The brothers stared at it for a moment, unsure of how to proceed. Then, Arjuna, ever the strategist, spoke up.

"Water flows, but it also wears down even the hardest stone over time," he said thoughtfully. "We cannot force our way through, but we can work with it."

Rishabh nodded. "Exactly, Arjuna. To master water, you must understand that force is not always the answer. Sometimes, yielding and adapting is the true path forward."

Arjuna knelt by the river, watching the way the water moved. His eyes traced the patterns of the current, studying how the water carved its path around obstacles. He stood up, and with a calm voice, instructed the others.

"We need to find the right path, the way the water will naturally guide us. We must flow with the river, not against it."

The brothers followed Arjuna's lead. They found rocks along the riverbank, which they used to create stepping stones, placing them strategically where the water was calmer. Slowly but surely, they crossed the river, each step more confident than the last. The lesson of water was clear: sometimes, the only way to overcome a challenge was to yield to its flow, to adapt and trust the process.

Rishabh smiled at their success. "You have passed the Trial of Water. Remember, in life, you will face many obstacles. But like water, you must learn to adapt, to bend and flow with circumstances, instead of resisting them."

The next trial lay in wait, and it was a test of fire. As they continued on their path, they came upon a clearing where a small fire burned in the center, surrounded by logs and embers. The fire crackled, sending sparks into the air.

"Fire is a force of transformation," Rishabh said, his voice now more intense. "It represents courage, passion, and the ability to transform what is into what could be. To pass the trial of fire, you must face your fears and transform them into strength."

The brothers looked at the fire with a sense of awe. Bhima, the strong one, was the first to step forward, but as he did, the fire flared up, almost as if it were challenging him. He hesitated, the heat from the flames stinging his skin.

"Bhima," Rishabh called, "do not fight the fire. To transform it, you must face it with courage and control, not force."

Bhima took a deep breath, closing his eyes and focusing on the heat. Instead of trying to overpower the flames, he let the fire's energy flow through him. He imagined his own fear as a burning ember and focused on transforming it, accepting the fire as part of him.

As Bhima stood firm, the flames seemed to settle, and the fire grew steady. His transformation was complete—he had learned that fire was not something to be feared, but something to be harnessed. The others followed his lead, each of them facing the flames in their own way, embracing the power of fire without being consumed by it.

"You have learned the lesson of fire," Rishabh said, his eyes glowing with pride. "Fire is courage and transformation. You must not fear the challenges that lie ahead, but face them with strength and the will to transform them into something greater."

Finally, Rishabh led the brothers to their last trial—the Trial of Air. They stood on a high cliff, the wind howling around them.

"Air represents freedom, clarity, and perspective," Rishabh said. "To pass this trial, you must rise above the confusion of the world and find clarity in your mind and heart. You must trust in the winds of destiny, and allow them to guide you."

The brothers felt the force of the wind pushing against them, yet they knew that this was not a battle to be fought, but a lesson to be learned. They stood still for a moment, feeling the wind rush past them. It was exhilarating, and yet, it carried with it a sense of peace.

Nakula, with his keen senses, was the first to close his eyes and let the wind flow around him. He felt the freedom it offered, the clarity it brought. The others followed, each finding their own connection to the air. The wind whispered to them, carrying with it the answers they had sought.

When they finally opened their eyes, they realized that they had passed the trial. The wind had taught them to see the world from a different perspective, to trust in the invisible forces that guided their path.

"You have learned the final lesson," Rishabh said, smiling warmly. "Air is clarity and freedom. With it, you will see your true path in life and trust that the winds will carry you toward your destiny."

The Pandavas had now faced all four elements—earth, water, fire, and air. They were no longer just brothers; they had become masters of nature's forces, each having learned invaluable lessons about resilience, adaptability, transformation, and clarity. With these lessons in their hearts, they were ready to face whatever challenges lay ahead.

As they stood together, looking out over the forest they had traversed, they knew that their journey was only just beginning. And no matter the trials, they would face them as one—stronger, wiser, and united.

Chapter 10: The Trial of the Heart

The lessons of the elements had forged the Pandavas into a stronger, more unified team. With the trials of earth, water, fire, and air behind them, they felt more connected to nature and to each other. Yet, Rishabh, their teacher, knew that the greatest challenge they would ever face was not in the forces of nature, but in the depths of their own hearts.

After the final trial of the elements, Rishabh took the brothers to a peaceful meadow, a place untouched by the harshness of life. The grass was soft beneath their feet, and the air was fragrant with the scent of blooming flowers. The sky above was a brilliant blue, dotted with the occasional cloud drifting lazily by.

"You have learned the lessons of the earth, water, fire, and air," Rishabh said, his voice filled with a calmness that matched the surroundings. "But now, we move to the most difficult trial of all: the Trial of the Heart."

The Pandavas, though filled with a sense of pride for overcoming the earlier trials, exchanged uneasy glances. What could this new trial involve? They had already faced physical challenges, mental challenges, and tests of their strength and adaptability. But the heart? The heart was not something easily tested.

Rishabh continued, sensing their confusion. "This trial will not test your physical strength or your ability to endure. It will test the strength of your hearts, the purity of your intentions, and the depth of your love for one another. For only with a pure heart can you overcome the darkness that will come in the future."

Yudhishthira, the eldest, spoke first. "What must we do to pass this trial, Rishabh?"

Rishabh smiled, his eyes thoughtful. "The heart speaks in many languages: compassion, sacrifice, forgiveness, and love. The trial before you is a journey within. You will each face your own fears, doubts, and desires, and only when you confront them with truth, will you pass the trial."

The Pandavas stood in silence, unsure of how to proceed. They had never been asked to face the heart in such a direct way. But Rishabh, understanding their uncertainty, stepped aside and gestured to the meadow.

"You will each find a path through the meadow," he explained. "Along that path, you will face illusions that will challenge your inner selves. You must walk the path alone, for this is a trial for each of you, individually. The first brother who reaches the end of the path will show the others the way. Only by facing your deepest fears and embracing your true selves will you be able to move forward."

With that, Rishabh stepped back, leaving the brothers to face their challenge. The meadow, though serene, now seemed to pulse with a strange energy, as if it too understood the significance of the trial.

Yudhishthira, being the eldest, was the first to step forward. He hesitated for a moment, his hand brushing the tall grass before him, and then he began walking. The path before him seemed to stretch endlessly, the edges of the meadow disappearing into a golden haze.

As he walked, Yudhishthira was suddenly surrounded by shadows, creeping up from the ground, whispering words of doubt and fear. The first shadow was his own guilt—his guilt over the choices he had made, the times when he had failed his brothers, his kingdom, and himself. The whispers in the shadows accused him of weakness, of being unfit to lead, of having failed as a son, a brother, and a king.

Yudhishthira's heart tightened. He had always tried to be just, to be fair, but the weight of responsibility had often felt like too much to bear. He stopped in his tracks, feeling the heavy burden of his doubts. The path in front of him seemed to grow darker.

But then, he remembered the lessons of the elements—the resilience of the earth, the flow of the water, the courage of the fire, and the clarity of the air. Yudhishthira closed his eyes and took a deep breath, steadying his mind. He remembered that he was not alone. He had his brothers, and they had always supported each other. They had faced many challenges together, and together they had triumphed.

He spoke to the shadows. "I am not perfect, and I have made mistakes. But I will not let my fears define me. I am a son of the Kuru dynasty, a brother to my family, and a king to my people. I will learn from my mistakes, and I will continue to fight for what is just."

As he spoke these words, the shadows began to fade, and the golden haze cleared. The path ahead became bright once again, and Yudhishthira moved forward, his heart lightened by his decision to face his fears.

Next, it was Bhima's turn. He stepped onto the path with his usual confidence, his broad shoulders strong and steady. But as he walked, the meadow around him began to change. The once calm air became thick with a choking smoke, and Bhima found himself in a dark, oppressive place. The smoke parted, and before him appeared an image of his father, Vayu, the god of wind.

"Bhima," the vision of his father said in a deep, rumbling voice, "You are strong, but your strength has often been your greatest weakness. You have been reckless, letting your emotions and rage guide you. Your fury has clouded your judgment, causing harm to those you love."

Bhima's fists clenched in anger, his pride wounded. He was a warrior, a protector, and no one had ever dared question his strength before. But deep down, he knew the truth of his father's words. He had allowed his anger to lead him, sometimes without thinking of the consequences. He had hurt those he cared for, even if unintentionally.

The smoky vision of Vayu spoke again, softer this time. "Strength without control is destruction. If you truly wish to protect those you love, you must first learn to master your emotions, to find peace within yourself."

Bhima's eyes softened. He knelt in the smoke and spoke, his voice steady and clear. "I have let my anger define me, but I will learn to control it. I will not let it consume me. I will protect my family, my kingdom, and my people, but I will do so with wisdom, not rage."

As he spoke, the smoke lifted, and the path before him became clear once more. Bhima stood tall, his heart lighter than before, and he continued his journey down the path.

The other brothers, one by one, faced their own trials—trials of doubt, guilt, desire, and fear. Nakula faced the shadow of vanity, Sahadeva confronted his fear of inadequacy, Arjuna faced the temptation of glory and fame, and each of them wrestled with their inner demons.

But like Yudhishthira and Bhima, they too found their strength in truth. They learned that the heart was not a force to be controlled, but a source of wisdom, love, and growth. It was not perfect, but it could be pure if one was willing to face the truth, no matter how painful.

At the end of the trial, all the brothers stood together once again, their hearts lighter and their spirits stronger. Rishabh, watching them with a proud smile, nodded.

"You have passed the Trial of the Heart," he said. "You are no longer just warriors; you are brothers bound by love and understanding. The journey ahead will be difficult, but with hearts full of truth, you will face whatever comes next with the strength of the elements and the wisdom of the heart."

The Pandavas knew that they were ready for whatever lay ahead. Their hearts were now pure, their bond unbreakable, and together, they would face their destiny with courage, compassion, and unwavering unity.

Chapter 11: The Whisper of Destiny

The days following the Trial of the Heart were filled with newfound clarity and strength for the Pandavas. The whispers of their fears, doubts, and desires had been silenced, and in their place stood a sense of unity and purpose. They had conquered their hearts, and now, it seemed as though the very universe itself was guiding them forward.

Rishabh, their mentor, noticed the change in them. No longer were they merely students of the elements, but they had become embodiments of the virtues each element represented. Yudhishthira, the embodiment of earth, stood firm and steady; Bhima, the embodiment of fire, burned with a controlled yet fierce passion; Arjuna, the embodiment of air, moved with speed and precision; Nakula, the embodiment of water, flowed with adaptability; and Sahadeva, the embodiment of light, illuminated the path with his wisdom.

Yet, Rishabh knew the time had come for them to learn the most critical lesson of all—one that would bind their destiny. It was time for them to understand the intricacies of dharma, the moral and spiritual code that governed not just their actions, but the entire cosmos.

One evening, as the sun began to set behind the tall mountains, casting an orange glow over the landscape, Rishabh called them together. He looked at each of them with great fondness, but also with a certain gravity, as though a weight hung upon his shoulders.

"Brothers," Rishabh began, "you have learned much, but there is one thing left to understand: the whisper of destiny. Every being, every event, every action has a purpose, and it is only by understanding that purpose that you can truly fulfill your role in this world."

Yudhishthira raised an eyebrow. "What do you mean, teacher? We are destined to do great things, but how do we know what our true purpose is?"

Rishabh smiled softly. "That, Yudhishthira, is the question each of you must answer in your own heart. Your dharma will reveal itself in time, but only if you remain true to your principles. But know this: Destiny is not a path that is given to you; it is a path you carve with your actions, your choices, and the way you choose to wield your virtues."

The Pandavas were quiet, each of them reflecting on the weight of Rishabh's words. Their hearts had been opened in ways they had never expected, and now they understood that their destiny was not something predetermined but something they had to shape with their lives.

"Teacher," Arjuna spoke up, his voice thoughtful. "If destiny is not already written, how do we know what is right? How do we ensure that our choices align with the greater good?"

Rishabh nodded, as though expecting the question. "Ah, Arjuna. This is the crux of dharma. Your choices must come from the heart, guided by wisdom, love, and justice. The moment you choose to act with righteousness, you are walking the path of your dharma. And remember, it is not always easy to distinguish the right choice. Sometimes, the right thing to do may seem unclear. But the purity of your intentions, the strength of your character, and the bond you share with your brothers will guide you toward the truth."

The air grew heavy with contemplation as the brothers mulled over Rishabh's teachings. It was clear that they were nearing the end of their training, but also the beginning of something much greater—something that could change not only their lives but the fate of their entire kingdom.

As the evening wore on, Rishabh spoke once more. "There is one more test for you, a test not of strength or wisdom, but of trust. You must trust each other completely, for it is only when you stand united that you will fulfill the greater purpose that lies ahead."

The brothers exchanged glances, understanding that their bond had been tested in many ways, but this new test would be different. It would ask them to rely on each other in ways they had never done before.

And so, as the stars began to twinkle in the night sky, Rishabh set the stage for their final lesson. "I will leave you with a challenge, one that will require you to face your deepest fears once again, but this time, together."

The brothers stepped forward, eager to understand what this final challenge would entail.

"Tomorrow," Rishabh said, "you will face a trial of trust. I will place each of you in separate situations, and you must rely on your brothers to help you. Trust in them completely, and only then will you be able to overcome the challenges set before you."

The brothers nodded in agreement. They had learned much from Rishabh, and though they knew this final trial would be difficult, they were ready to face it together. As they went to bed that night, each of them found themselves reflecting on the lesson they had just received.

For the first time, they understood that destiny was not a destination, but a journey—a journey that was shaped by the choices they made and the trust they placed in each other. And together, they were ready to face whatever came next.

The following day dawned bright and clear, the first rays of sunlight stretching across the land. As Rishabh prepared them for their final trial, he spoke softly but firmly.

"Remember, it is not enough to be strong alone. It is not enough to be wise alone. It is not enough to be just alone. Your true power lies in your ability to trust one another, for it is through unity that you will fulfill your true purpose."

With those words, the Pandavas set out on their final trial, knowing that their destiny would soon unfold in ways they had never imagined. And as they walked toward the unknown, they did so not as individuals, but as a united force, bound together by love, trust, and the unbreakable bond of brotherhood.

Chapter 12: The Trial of Trust

The sun was high in the sky as the Pandavas gathered at the edge of the forest, their hearts filled with anticipation and a little anxiety. Rishabh had spoken of a test—a test that would push them not only to face their fears but to completely rely on one another. Today, they would learn whether their bond of brotherhood could withstand the weight of their shared destiny.

Rishabh stood before them, his gaze steady, his voice calm. "The Trial of Trust will test you in ways you cannot imagine. You must trust in each other completely, without question. In this trial, each of you will be placed in a separate challenge. You will not be able to see one another, but you will be able to communicate. It is through your bond that you will succeed or fail."

The brothers exchanged looks of concern. They had faced countless challenges, but this trial was different. It was not about defeating an external enemy or mastering a skill. It was about trusting each other in a way that transcended everything they had learned so far.

Rishabh continued. "The test begins now. I will give each of you a task. You must call upon your brothers for help, and they must come to your aid without hesitation. Do not doubt them, for doubt will only lead to failure. Trust is the foundation of this trial, and the very core of your dharma."

With that, Rishabh gestured for them to spread out, and the Pandavas began their journey into the forest, each facing an obstacle designed to test their trust in one another.

Yudhishthira's Trial: The Mirror of Truth

Yudhishthira, the eldest of the Pandavas, found himself standing before a large mirror set in the heart of the forest. It was a strange sight, for the mirror was not like any he had seen before. It shimmered with a strange light, and as he gazed into it, he saw his reflection—but not as he was now. The image before him was that of a king, crowned and regal, surrounded by wealth and power.

However, the image quickly twisted, and Yudhishthira saw himself surrounded by enemies, his kingdom crumbling to dust. He watched as the mirror displayed moments of shame, doubt, and regret. His heart tightened with fear.

The mirror whispered, "What if you fail? What if your actions lead to the ruin of your kingdom? Can you live with the consequences of your choices?"

Yudhishthira's mind swirled with doubt, but then he remembered Rishabh's words. Trust. Trust in himself, and trust in his brothers. He knew that he was not alone—his brothers stood with him, and together, they would overcome anything.

He closed his eyes and spoke aloud, calling for Bhima. "Bhima, come to me. I need your strength."

At that moment, the mirror began to shudder, its image flickering as Bhima appeared from the shadows, his presence a comforting force. Bhima placed his hand on Yudhishthira's shoulder, and together, they faced the mirror once again. The image of doubt faded, and Yudhishthira saw a vision of himself, wise and just, leading his people with honor.

"Thank you, Bhima," Yudhishthira said, his voice steady once more. "Together, we will succeed."

Bhima's Trial: The Raging Fire

Bhima's trial was no less daunting. He stood before a vast chasm, its depths filled with swirling flames. The fire roared, threatening to engulf him, but Bhima was not afraid. He knew his strength and his power, and he had always believed that he could overcome any challenge on his own.

However, as he stepped forward, the fire grew fiercer. The heat was unbearable, and Bhima found himself faltering. The flames twisted around him, whispering dark thoughts into his mind. "You are strong, but not strong enough. You cannot face this alone."

For a moment, Bhima hesitated. He had always prided himself on his strength, but now he realized that brute force would not be enough. He called out to Nakula, his voice urgent. "Nakula, I need your help. The fire is too great for me alone."

Nakula appeared beside him without hesitation, his calm demeanor a stark contrast to the raging flames. Nakula, the embodiment of water, raised his hands and began to chant a prayer. Slowly, the fire began to subside, its heat diminishing as Nakula summoned the power of water to quell the flames.

Bhima's eyes widened with realization. "I could not have done this without you, Nakula. Thank you."

Arjuna's Trial: The Blindfolded Archer

Arjuna's trial was a test of precision and skill. He found himself standing on a cliff, a bow in hand, facing a target far in the distance. The target was small and seemingly impossible to hit, but Arjuna was the greatest archer in the world. He had complete faith in his abilities.

However, as he aimed his bow, a heavy blindfold was placed over his eyes. The world went dark. He could hear the sounds of the forest around him—the rustling of leaves, the chirping of birds—but he could not see the target.

A voice from nowhere spoke. "Can you hit your mark without sight? Your strength lies not in your eyes, but in your heart. Do you trust your brothers enough to guide you?"

Arjuna stood still, breathing deeply. He knew he could not do this alone. He called out to Sahadeva. "Sahadeva, guide me. I cannot do this without your wisdom."

Sahadeva appeared, his voice calm and sure. "Focus, Arjuna. I will guide you. Trust in my words."

Arjuna steadied his breath and drew the bowstring, listening intently to Sahadeva's instructions. With perfect alignment, he released the arrow. It flew through the air and struck the target dead center.

"Together, we are unstoppable," Arjuna said, his heart swelling with gratitude.

Nakula's Trial: The Illusion of the Heart

Nakula's trial took a different form. He found himself walking through a beautiful garden, filled with vibrant flowers and sweet fragrances. But as he ventured deeper into the garden, he noticed something strange—the flowers began to wilt, the trees began to wither, and the sky grew dark.

A voice echoed in the air, "This garden is a reflection of your heart, Nakula. You see beauty in everything, but can you accept the darkness that lies within?"

Nakula paused, feeling a sense of unease settle over him. He had always been the calm and composed one, but this trial tested him in ways he had never anticipated.

He called out to his brothers, but it was Arjuna's voice that reached him first. "Nakula, you must not run from the darkness. Embrace it, for only then can you bring back the light."

Nakula closed his eyes and breathed deeply, focusing on his inner strength. As he opened his eyes, the darkness began to recede, replaced once more by the light of the garden.

"Thank you, Arjuna," Nakula whispered, realizing that true strength came not from ignoring the darkness but from accepting it.

Sahadeva's Trial: The Choice of the Soul

Sahadeva's trial was the most subtle, yet the most profound. He stood at the edge of a vast river, its waters flowing steadily. On the other side of the river stood a vision of his future—a future filled with glory, respect, and the fulfillment of his destiny.

Yet, the river was wide and deep. To cross it, Sahadeva would need to leave behind everything he had known. The voice of destiny called to him, urging him to cross, to embrace the path that awaited him.

But Sahadeva hesitated. "Is this truly my path? Or is it a dream of destiny that does not belong to me?"

It was at that moment that his brothers appeared, standing side by side. "We are with you, Sahadeva," they said in unison. "You do not need to walk alone. The river is wide, but together, we can cross it."

Sahadeva smiled, his heart lightened by their presence. Together, they crossed the river, each of them stepping into the unknown, trusting that their bond would carry them forward.

The End of the Trial

As the Pandavas reunited, they found themselves stronger than ever before. Each of them had faced their own fear, their own challenge, and had come to understand the true meaning of trust. It was not just about relying on one another in times of need; it was about recognizing that together, they were more powerful than they could ever be alone.

Rishabh stood before them, his eyes filled with pride. "You have passed the Trial of Trust. You now understand that your destiny is not a solitary path, but one that is shaped by the strength of your bond. As you move forward, remember this: when you trust one another, there is no obstacle you cannot overcome."

With their hearts full and their spirits united, the Pandavas were ready for whatever challenges lay ahead. They had learned the most valuable lesson of all—that together, they were unstoppable.

Chapter 13: The Path of Dharma

The dawn broke softly over the hills as the Pandavas gathered on the banks of the sacred river. The serene waters reflected the colors of the rising sun, casting a calm glow on the group. They stood in silence, each contemplating the events that had brought them to this point. The trials they had endured had strengthened their bond, but Rishabh had made it clear that the journey was far from over.

Rishabh, ever the guide, stood before them, his expression serious yet reassuring. "The next lesson you must learn is one of the most important of all—the path of Dharma. It is the foundation upon which your actions must rest. Without it, even the strongest of warriors can lose their way."

Yudhishthira, the eldest, looked at Rishabh with curiosity. "What is Dharma, Master? We have heard this word many times, but we do not fully understand it."

Rishabh smiled and nodded. "Dharma is the righteous path, the moral law that governs the universe. It is the code of conduct that guides every action, thought, and word. It is not something that can be taught in a single lesson— it must be understood through experience and reflection."

The Pandavas were eager to learn. They had already learned the importance of trust, strength, and unity. Now, it was time to understand the deeper forces that shaped their world and the responsibilities that came with their destiny.

Rishabh continued, "To understand Dharma, you must first understand your role in the world. You are not just princes or warriors—you are protectors of the people, upholders of justice, and keepers of the truth. Every action you take must reflect these responsibilities. You must always act with righteousness, even when it is difficult."

The wind rustled through the trees, and the sound of the river's flow seemed to echo Rishabh's words. The Pandavas stood in quiet contemplation. They had already faced great challenges, but the path of Dharma was something new, something profound. They knew it would take all their strength to uphold it.

Yudhishthira's Lesson: The Test of Leadership

Yudhishthira, as the eldest, felt the weight of his family's future on his shoulders. He knew that his actions would set the example for his brothers and for the kingdom he was destined to lead. Yet, the path of Dharma was not always clear. Sometimes, the right decision was not the easiest one, and it required a great deal of courage to follow.

One day, while traveling through a neighboring village, the Pandavas came upon a crowd gathered around a dispute. A poor farmer, his clothes ragged and his face lined with worry, stood before the village chief. The farmer had lost his crops to a storm, and now the chief demanded payment for a debt the farmer could not afford to repay.

Yudhishthira stepped forward, his heart heavy with the plight of the farmer. He listened to both sides carefully before speaking. "The farmer has lost everything. It is not his fault that the storm destroyed his crops. I will speak with the chief and request that the debt be forgiven."

But the chief, a proud man, refused to listen. "The law is the law, and it must be followed. If the farmer does not pay, he will face punishment."

Yudhishthira stood tall. "The law cannot be blind to the circumstances of each case. Dharma requires us to show compassion, especially in times of hardship. A wise leader knows when to be firm and when to show mercy."

The chief, moved by Yudhishthira's words and presence, reluctantly agreed to forgive the farmer's debt. The villagers, witnessing this act of compassion, praised Yudhishthira for his wisdom and fairness.

Yudhishthira turned to his brothers, a sense of fulfillment in his heart. "Dharma is not about following rules blindly. It is about understanding the needs of the people and making decisions that benefit all, even when it is difficult."

Bhima's Lesson: The Strength of Compassion

For Bhima, the lesson of Dharma was tied to his strength. He had always prided himself on his immense physical power, but Rishabh had warned him that strength alone was not enough to lead a kingdom or to live a righteous life. It was what lay behind the strength that mattered—compassion and the will to protect those who could not protect themselves.

One afternoon, while exploring a dense part of the forest, Bhima came across a wounded animal—a deer, its leg caught in a hunter's trap. The creature struggled, its eyes wide with fear and pain. Bhima's natural instinct was to kill the hunter who had set the trap, but something inside him paused. The deer was innocent, and it was not the fault of the animal that it had been caught.

Bhima knelt down and carefully freed the animal from the trap. He gently cradled it in his strong arms, offering it water and comfort. As he did, he thought about the true nature of strength. It was not enough to wield power in battle. Strength should be used to protect the helpless, to show mercy to those who could not defend themselves.

When the deer had recovered, it bounded off into the forest, free once more. Bhima stood, his heart swelling with pride. "True strength," he thought, "is not in what you can destroy, but in what you can save."

Arjuna's Lesson: The Choice Between Duty and Desire

Arjuna's journey along the path of Dharma was not without its struggles. As a great archer, he had always sought excellence in his craft. But now, Rishabh had asked him to face the deeper question of duty versus desire.

One evening, Arjuna found himself alone in the forest, practicing with his bow. He was lost in his thoughts, perfecting his aim and technique. But as he focused on his target, a voice called out to him from the shadows.

It was Krishna, the charioteer of the Pandavas, who had been observing him. "Arjuna, your skill with the bow is unparalleled. But what is it you seek? Victory in battle? Glory? Or something deeper?"

Arjuna paused, the question striking at his heart. "I seek victory, Master. I wish to be the greatest warrior who ever lived."

Krishna smiled. "Victory and glory are fleeting, Arjuna. They are desires that can never be fully satisfied. But duty—duty to your people, to your family, and to righteousness—is something that endures beyond time. It is the essence of Dharma."

Krishna continued, "When you fight, do not do so for personal gain. Fight because it is your duty to protect those who cannot protect themselves. When you aim your bow, let it be for the cause of justice, not for the glory of your name."

Arjuna nodded, his heart heavy with understanding. "I will remember this, Krishna. It is not victory I seek, but righteousness."

Nakula and Sahadeva's Lesson: The Balance of the Heart

Nakula and Sahadeva, the twin brothers, had always worked in harmony, their strengths complementing each other. Yet, they, too, had to learn the balance of Dharma—the balance between their individual desires and their shared responsibilities.

One day, as they traveled together through the forest, they came upon a group of people who had been displaced by a flood. The people were hungry and tired, their faces drawn with despair. Nakula, ever the optimist, wished to help them, offering them food and shelter. Sahadeva, ever the realist, knew that resources were limited and feared that helping the refugees might stretch their own provisions too thin.

They argued for a time, each standing firm in his beliefs. But then, as they looked into the eyes of the people, they realized that their duty was clear. The balance of Dharma lay in their ability to give without depleting themselves entirely.

Nakula smiled and said, "We will help them, but we will also make sure that we do not harm our own people in the process."

Sahadeva agreed, and together, they found a way to help the refugees while ensuring that their own people would not suffer.

The Conclusion of the Lesson

As the sun set that evening, the Pandavas gathered once more by the river. They had each faced their own challenges along the path of Dharma and had learned that it was not a simple or easy journey. It was a lifelong pursuit, requiring constant reflection, compassion, and balance.

Rishabh stood before them, his eyes proud. "You have learned much, my children. Dharma is not a path that is always clear, but it is the path that will guide you through the darkness. It will be your strength in times of doubt, your shield in times of conflict, and your light in times of despair."

The Pandavas, now wiser and stronger, understood that the journey ahead would be long and filled with many challenges. But as long as they remained true to the path of Dharma, they would always find their way.

With hearts full of purpose, they set off once more, ready for the trials and triumphs that lay ahead. Together, they would walk the path of righteousness, knowing that it was the only path that truly mattered.

Chapter 14: The Echo of Fate

The sun dipped lower in the sky, casting long shadows over the Pandavas as they ventured deeper into the forest. The journey ahead was still uncertain, and although they had learned the path of Dharma, the true test of their strength was yet to come. Rishabh had prepared them for many challenges, but none of them were prepared for what the future held.

The winds whispered through the trees, carrying with them a sense of foreboding. Yudhishthira, ever the thoughtful leader, sensed that a great trial was approaching. He had learned to listen to the signs of the world around him, and his instincts told him that their peace was about to be shattered.

As the brothers made camp for the night, they gathered around the fire, the flickering flames casting an orange glow on their faces. Rishabh sat silently beside them, his eyes closed in meditation. Yudhishthira turned to him, his voice low but steady. "Master, what do you foresee in our future? What challenges await us on this journey?"

Rishabh opened his eyes, his gaze distant yet sharp. "The winds of fate are shifting, Yudhishthira. The time will soon come when your courage and wisdom will be tested in ways you cannot yet imagine. Forces beyond your control are gathering, and the choices you make will determine the future of your kingdom and your family."

Arjuna, his bow resting beside him, looked up with concern. "Master, we have already faced many challenges, and we have learned much from you. Are we not ready for what lies ahead?"

Rishabh's expression remained calm, though his words carried a weight of truth. "It is not enough to simply be ready, Arjuna. The trials that will come will test not just your strength, but your spirit, your bond as brothers, and your loyalty to the truth. The enemy you face will not always be visible, and the greatest battles may not be fought with weapons."

The fire crackled in the silence that followed, and the brothers exchanged uneasy glances. They had learned much about Dharma and had become stronger together, but the ominous words of Rishabh weighed heavily on their hearts.

Bhima's Strength Tested

The next morning, as the sun rose over the horizon, the Pandavas continued their journey, their path leading them deeper into the heart of the forest. As they crossed a narrow bridge over a swiftly flowing river, they encountered a massive beast—a Rakshasa, a demon of great power, blocking their way.

The creature towered over them, its eyes glowing with malice. "None shall pass without facing me!" it bellowed, its voice like thunder, shaking the very earth beneath their feet.

Bhima, his blood boiling with the desire for battle, stepped forward, his fists clenched. "We are the sons of King Pandu! You will not stop us from our journey."

The Rakshasa laughed cruelly. "I have defeated many warriors stronger than you. Do you truly believe you can defeat me, mere children of man?"

The brothers stood their ground, but Bhima's rage flared. He charged at the demon, his massive form like a storm of fury. The Rakshasa's claws slashed at him, but Bhima was swift, his power unmatched. Blow after blow, Bhima struck with all his might, but the demon was resilient, its body as hard as iron.

Finally, Bhima, with one powerful punch, landed a blow to the demon's chest. The Rakshasa staggered and fell, its roar echoing through the forest before it vanished into the mist. The Pandavas stood victorious, but the victory was bittersweet. Bhima, though proud of his strength, knew that true strength was not only in physical power. The challenge had reminded him of the importance of wisdom in battle—something Rishabh had taught him well.

Arjuna's Moment of Doubt

The next trial came in the form of doubt—a shadow that seemed to cloud Arjuna's mind. As the brothers continued their journey, they came upon a majestic temple, its spires reaching toward the heavens. Inside, the walls were adorned with intricate carvings of gods and warriors. But amidst the beauty, Arjuna found himself lost in thought, wondering if his path had truly been chosen for him.

One evening, as the brothers rested, Arjuna wandered away from the camp, his heart troubled by questions he could not answer. He walked through the temple, his fingers brushing against the carvings, each image a reminder of his legacy. His mind raced—had he chosen the right path? Was he truly a servant of Dharma, or had his ambitions blinded him to his true purpose?

In the silence of the temple, Krishna appeared, his presence as soothing as the night sky. "Arjuna," he said, his voice soft yet clear, "why do you walk in solitude, burdened by doubt?"

Arjuna turned to Krishna, his eyes troubled. "I question my place in the world, Krishna. I have always sought to be the greatest archer, the greatest warrior. But in my pursuit of glory, have I lost sight of what truly matters?"

Krishna smiled gently, his words full of wisdom. "You have chosen a path of great responsibility, Arjuna. But remember this: greatness is not measured by how many victories you achieve, but by how you serve others, by how you use your talents for the greater good. The true measure of a warrior is not his skill with weapons, but his ability to fight for justice, to fight for truth, to fight for Dharma."

Arjuna's heart eased, the weight of his doubts lifting. "Thank you, Krishna. Your words remind me of the true path I must walk."

The Test of Unity: The Brothers' Bond

As the days passed, the Pandavas faced further challenges, each one testing their unity as brothers. Whether it was overcoming natural obstacles or helping the people they encountered, they learned that the strength of their bond was their greatest weapon. The more they worked together, the more they understood the true meaning of Dharma.

One day, as they rested near a river, Rishabh called them together. "The trials you have faced so far have been important, but now comes the greatest challenge of all. It is the test of unity. You are bound together not just by blood, but by purpose. The bond you share is what will carry you through the darkest times. Never forget that."

The Pandavas stood silently, understanding the depth of Rishabh's words. They had each learned valuable lessons, but it was their shared destiny that would ultimately define their journey.

The Echo of Fate

As the moon rose high in the sky, casting its silver light over the forest, the Pandavas continued on their journey. Their hearts were filled with wisdom, and their spirits strong, but they could not shake the sense that fate was drawing them toward something greater. The challenges they had faced so far had prepared them for what was to come, but they knew that the trials ahead would be even more difficult.

Rishabh's words echoed in their minds, reminding them that true strength was not in their weapons or their abilities, but in their unity, their faith in Dharma, and their commitment to righteousness. The brothers, though young, had already come to understand that their destiny was intertwined with the fate of their kingdom and their people. It was a destiny that would require courage, sacrifice, and unwavering loyalty to the path of righteousness.

And so, they walked on—toward a future unknown, yet certain in their hearts that together, they could face whatever trials lay ahead. The echo of fate was loud in their ears, but they were not afraid. For as long as they stood united, there was no force in the world that could break them.

Chapter 15: The Path to Destiny

The journey of the Pandavas had brought them far from the comforts of their palace, and with each step, they had grown stronger, wiser, and more connected to the world around them. The trials they faced had sharpened their minds and tested their hearts, but now they found themselves at a crossroads. The forest, once a place of mystery and adventure, had become a place of deep reflection. It was here, in this sacred space, that their ultimate test awaited.

Rishabh, their guide and teacher, sat calmly beneath a large banyan tree, his eyes closed as he meditated. The air was thick with anticipation, as though the very earth itself was holding its breath. The Pandavas, now fully aware of the gravity of their mission, gathered around him. They had learned much, but now they stood on the threshold of something far greater than any lesson could prepare them for.

Yudhishthira, ever the leader, approached Rishabh first. "Master," he said, his voice filled with resolve, "We have faced many trials, and with each, we have become stronger. But what lies ahead is still unclear to us. What do we do now?"

Rishabh opened his eyes slowly, his gaze soft yet piercing. "The path you are about to walk is not one of simple victories, Yudhishthira. It is a path that will test your very essence. The time has come for you to stand before your destiny and choose the future you will create."

Arjuna stepped forward, his mind racing with thoughts of the challenges yet to come. "Master, we know the value of strength, but what of wisdom? What if we are tested beyond our limits? What if our choices lead us down a path of destruction?"

Rishabh nodded, understanding the concern in Arjuna's voice. "Wisdom is the beacon that will guide you through the storm. But remember, it is not always the path of least resistance that leads to greatness. Sometimes, the greatest wisdom lies in making the hardest choices, those that require sacrifice for the greater good."

Bhima, who had always been driven by his immense physical strength, spoke next. "But Master, we have fought with our strength for so long. How will we overcome the trials ahead if not with our might?"

Rishabh's expression softened as he regarded Bhima. "Strength, Bhima, is not only in your muscles. True strength lies in your heart. The path ahead will require not just physical might but moral courage. It will ask you to fight not only for victory but for justice, truth, and the welfare of others. Your strength will be measured by your ability to stand for what is right, even when it is the hardest thing to do."

The brothers stood in silence, taking in Rishabh's words. They had come to realize that their journey was not just one of physical battles and victories. It was a journey of growth, of learning to balance their inner strengths with their responsibilities as future leaders. They had come to understand that the path of Dharma was not always clear, but it was a path that would require them to face their fears, their doubts, and their own weaknesses.

The Appearance of Duryodhana

As the brothers continued to reflect on their path, a shadow fell over them. From the trees emerged a figure, tall and imposing—Duryodhana, the eldest son of Dhritarashtra, and the brother to their cousins, the Kauravas. His face was set in a cold expression, his eyes burning with a mix of pride and anger. He had long coveted the throne of Hastinapura, and his animosity toward the Pandavas was well known.

"Ah, the mighty Pandavas," Duryodhana sneered, "how grand you have become. But remember this—you are no more than the children of Pandu, and I will ensure that you remain nothing more."

Yudhishthira stepped forward, his demeanor calm but firm. "Duryodhana, your words mean little to us. We seek only the path of righteousness, not power. Our duty is to the people of Hastinapura, to our kingdom, and to Dharma. You may try to thwart us, but the path we walk is destined, and no force can change it."

Duryodhana's eyes flashed with anger. "Your destiny is one that will see you defeated. You may have wisdom, strength, and unity, but it is ambition that will ultimately destroy you. You cannot defeat me, for I will stop at nothing to claim what I believe is rightfully mine."

Bhima, ever ready for a challenge, clenched his fists, his anger rising. "We shall see about that, Duryodhana. You speak of ambition, but it is your greed and hatred that will be your downfall. We will not bow to you."

But Rishabh, sensing the danger of the moment, raised a hand. "Enough," he said, his voice calm but authoritative. "Duryodhana's words come from a heart clouded by pride. You must not be swayed by his anger. Remember, true victory lies not in defeating your enemy, but in overcoming your own desires and fears."

Duryodhana, seeing that his words had failed to provoke the Pandavas, turned and walked away, his steps heavy with frustration. As he disappeared into the forest, the Pandavas stood in silence, the weight of the encounter settling over them. They knew that this was only the beginning of a much larger conflict—one that would not be won by force alone, but by wisdom, unity, and an unwavering commitment to Dharma.

The Final Test

As the days passed, the Pandavas continued their journey, their bond growing stronger with each challenge they overcame. Rishabh, though ever calm, continued to remind them of their true mission—to prepare for the trials that would define their legacy. The final test, he told them, was yet to come.

One evening, as the sun dipped below the horizon, casting a golden glow over the land, Rishabh gathered the brothers once more. "You have learned much, but there is one final lesson that you must understand. The greatest challenge you will face is not the one that lies outside of you, but the one within. It is the test of your inner strength—the strength to make the right choices, even when the path is unclear, even when the stakes are high."

Yudhishthira, ever the seeker of truth, looked at Rishabh with determination. "We are ready, Master. Whatever the future holds, we will face it together, as brothers, as servants of Dharma."

Rishabh smiled, a proud look in his eyes. "You are ready, Yudhishthira. The world will test you in ways you cannot yet understand. But know this: as long as you stay true to your purpose, as long as you walk the path of righteousness, you will fulfill your destiny. The Pandavas are not just sons of Pandu—they are the bearers of a legacy that will shape the future of the world."

With those final words, Rishabh rose to his feet, his gaze set on the horizon. The brothers stood in silence, each feeling the weight of his words and the enormity of their mission. They were no longer just children of the royal family—they were the future of Hastinapura, the protectors of Dharma, and the stewards of a legacy that would define their people for generations to come.

And so, with hearts filled with resolve, the Pandavas continued on their journey. Their path was uncertain, their trials yet to unfold, but one thing was clear: the bond they shared, the lessons they had learned, and the strength of their spirit would carry them through whatever lay ahead. For they were the Pandavas, and their destiny was to shape the future of the world itself.

Conclusion: The Unbroken Legacy

The journey of the Pandavas, from their humble beginnings in the forests to the throne of Hastinapura, was one not just of physical battles but of spiritual growth, moral decisions, and personal transformation. It was a journey that tested their courage, unity, and commitment to Dharma—the sacred duty that defined their very existence.

Throughout their challenges, the Pandavas faced trials that tested their resolve. They encountered adversaries who sought to destroy them, temptations that threatened to pull them off course, and moments of doubt that made them question their path. Yet, it was in these moments of adversity that they found their true strength—not in their weapons or their might, but in their hearts, their wisdom, and the power of their bond as brothers. Their journey was not defined by the battles they fought but by the virtues they upheld: righteousness, truth, justice, and sacrifice.

Yudhishthira, the eldest of the Pandavas, embodied the essence of wisdom and moral fortitude. His unwavering commitment to truth and Dharma guided his brothers through their darkest moments. Arjuna, the greatest of archers, represented the pursuit of excellence, mastering not just his skills but his own inner conflicts. Bhima, with his immense strength, taught the importance of fighting for justice, not for vengeance. Nakula and Sahadeva, the twins, embodied the values of loyalty, humility, and compassion. Together, they stood united, proving that strength is not measured by individual power but by the unity of purpose and the collective effort of those who walk the path of righteousness.

Their journey was also a reminder of the complexities of life and leadership. Even the mightiest heroes faced moral dilemmas, and the choices they made shaped their destinies. The Pandavas learned that leadership was not about ruling with force but with fairness, compassion, and a deep sense of responsibility toward those they served. They were not just princes—they were protectors of their people, guardians of Dharma, and embodiments of hope for the future.

The lessons they learned were not just for themselves, but for all who would follow in their footsteps. Their story was a testament to the power of perseverance, the importance of unity, and the enduring strength of values that transcend time and space. The Pandavas' legacy would go on to shape the future, not because they were the most powerful or the most victorious, but because they upheld the highest ideals in the face of adversity.

And though their story is one of the past, their lessons remain timeless. The Pandavas show us that true strength lies in the heart, that wisdom must guide our actions, and that the greatest battles we face are often those within ourselves. Their legacy reminds us that no matter how difficult the journey, if we stay true to our purpose and walk the path of righteousness, we too can overcome any challenge.

The story of the Pandavas is more than just a tale of kings and warriors—it is a beacon of light, a call to live with honor, and a reminder that even in the face of darkness, the pursuit of truth and justice will always guide us to the light.

Made in United States
Troutdale, OR
12/04/2024

25894282R00046